History's Fearless Fighters

SPARTANS

Rupert
Matthews

Gareth Stevens
PUBLISHING

Please visit our website, **www.garethstevens.com**.
For a free color catalog of all our high-quality books, call toll free 1-800-542-2595 or fax 1-877-542-2596

Library of Congress Cataloging-in-Publication Data

Matthews, Rupert.
Spartans / by Rupert Matthews.
p. cm. — (History's fearless fighters)
Includes index.
ISBN 978-1-4824-3181-0 (pbk.)
ISBN 978-1-4824-3184-1 (6 pack)
ISBN 978-1-4824-3182-7 (library binding)
1. Sparta (Extinct city) — History, Military — Juvenile literature.
2. Soldiers — Greece — Sparta (Extinct city) — Juvenile literature.
I. Matthews, Rupert. II. Title.
DF261.S8 M38 2016
938'.9—d23

First Edition

Published in 2016 by
Gareth Stevens Publishing
111 East 14th Street, Suite 349
New York, NY 10003

© Alix Wood Books

Produced for Gareth Stevens by Alix Wood Books
Designed by Alix Wood
Editor: Eloise Macgregor

Photo credits:
Cover, 3, 27 bottom, 40 © istock; 1, © Shutterstock/Rama; 4, 5 middle, 6, 7 bottom, 10, 15, 16, 18, 20, 22, 26, 33, 36, 43 © Shutterstock; 5 top, 28 © Alix Wood; 5 bottom © Ronny Siegel; 7 top, 13, 30, 37 top, 42 bottom © DollarPhotoClub; 14 © Fotolia; 17 © Berthold Werner; 19 bottom © Spartan Warriors, 2004, Howard David Johnson; 21 top © INTERFOTO/Alamy; 21 © Tom Old; 23 top, 37 bottom © The Trustees of the British Museum; 23 bottom © riproduzioni storiche, 24 © Museum of Fine Arts, Boston; 27 top © Marsyas; 32 © Tate Britain, 34 © Herbert Ortner; 41 © Metropolitan Museum of Art; remaining images are in the public domain

Printed in the United States of America
CPSIA compliance information: Batch #CS15GS: For further information contact Gareth Stevens, New York, New York at 1-800-542-2595.

Contents

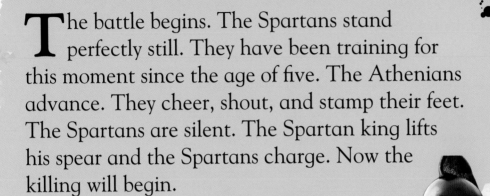

The battle begins. The Spartans stand perfectly still. They have been training for this moment since the age of five. The Athenians advance. They cheer, shout, and stamp their feet. The Spartans are silent. The Spartan king lifts his spear and the Spartans charge. Now the killing will begin.

The Spartan army was the most feared fighting force in Greece, perhaps even in the world! The training that the Spartans went through was intense and never-ending. Men aged 60 or 70 years old trained and fought alongside men of 18 or 20 years old. So long as a Spartan could march, he fought in the army.

That's Fearless!

Spartan soldiers were told to return "with your shield, or on it." Men who were killed were dragged home on their shields. The saying meant "come back victorious or dead."

Sparta was a small city in southern Greece. It ruled the valley of the Eurotas River and later the Pamisos River valley as well.

Southern Europe showing Sparta

Spartan Territory

Only the men from a small number of families were allowed to join the army. Everyone else was forced to work and pay heavy taxes to support the army, nobles, and kings.

There is not much left of Sparta today. Unlike most Greeks, the Spartans did not build large temples, theaters or houses. Spartans had simple temples made of wood and preferred to live simply in wooden houses

Sparta as it looks now

Three Nations in One

The Spartan state was made up of three separate groups of people; **Spartiates**, **periokoi**, and **helots**. All were essential to the Spartan army, although only one group did the actual fighting. The group system was designed by the royal prince Lycurgus in about 770 BCE. The Spartans believed it was the best way to win wars.

Only Spartiates were allowed to join the army. They were banned from doing any other job. Spartiates owned all the land in Sparta. They were the only people allowed to vote in elections or serve in government. The two royal families of Sparta were Spartiates. There were 9,000 other Spartiate families.

a Helot

a Spartiate

The periokoi were allowed to work in any job they liked - as farmers, merchants, potters, or blacksmiths - but they were not allowed to join the army or to vote. Some periokoi were very rich, but they all had to pay taxes to the government to pay for the army. Some foreigners from outside Sparta were allowed to settle and become periokoi.

DANGEROUS BIRTH

When a male Spartiate was born, his father had to show him to the elders. If the baby had any disability or looked weak he was taken to the slopes of Mount Taygetos and left to die. If he looked strong he was taken home. The baby was then bathed in wine to make him even stronger!

The helots were little better than slaves. They lived on farms and estates owned by the Spartiates and were forced to work. Helots were allowed to worship the gods, unlike most slaves in ancient Greece. They could also do some work for themselves, and keep any money they made. Helots did go to war, but only as servants, cooks, and to carry food and weapons.

Helots were forced to wear a hat made out of dog skin to show they were slaves! If a helot earned enough money to become a periokoi he was allowed to wear a woolen cap with a pointed top to show everyone that he had become free.

Mount Taygetos

Chosen to Fight

At the age of five, Spartan boys left their family home to go and live in army barracks. In the barracks they began to learn the skills of fighting, but they were also given a full education. The boys had to learn how to read and write, do math, and learn the history of Sparta.

Each boy was given a child-sized helmet and shield that he had to carry at all times to get used to their weight. At the age of 10 the young Spartan began to learn special exercises that involved dancing, singing, playing musical instruments, and athletics. He had to learn songs written by the poet Tyrtaios. These songs included marching songs that helped the men keep in step. Other songs told the stories of brave heroes, or gave advice on how to fight in battle.

A PARTY SONG

An excerpt from a song by Tyrtaios sung at parties:

Let a man learn how to fight by first
  daring to perform mighty deeds,
Not where the missiles won't reach,
  if he is armed with a shield,
But getting in close where fighting is
  hand to hand, inflicting a wound
With his long spear or his sword,
  taking the enemy's life,
With his foot planted alongside a
  foot and his shield pressed against
  shield embroiled in the action—
  let him fight man to man,
Holding secure in his grasp haft of
  his sword or his spear!

Spartan girls stayed at home, but unlike in most Greek states, the girls were given an education and encouraged to take part in sports competitions. They were given the same food as the boys and could wear whatever clothes they liked. In other countries, girls were given poor food and forced to cover themselves in thick cloaks and veils. Adult women could own property and speak in political debates, but could not vote.

A painting by Christoffer Wilhelm Eckersberg of young Spartans learning archery

That's Fearless!

The first thing a five-year old boy had to learn was how to perform the **pyrriche** dance. This was a dangerous dance that involved juggling and catching razor-sharp weapons while singing a special song.

Training Young Fighters

At the age of 12, Spartan boys were tested in their skills with weapons, athletics, singing, and dancing. If he passed the tests, a boy was given the rank of "youth" in the barracks. Life for a youth was very uncomfortable. It was designed to make the youth strong and tough so that he would be an effective soldier. The training system was called "the **agoge**."

Youths were allowed to wear only one thing - a woolen cloak. They were not allowed any shoes, hats, or underwear. No matter how hot or cold the weather, the youth had to have his cloak and was punished if he wore anything else. His bed was made of dried rushes that he picked himself. In winter he was allowed to mix thistledown into the rushes for added warmth.

BLACK SOUP

Dinner every day consisted of Spartan black soup. It was made by boiling pork and barley in pig's blood mixed with vinegar and salt. A man from the city of Sybaris ate some black soup and then said "Now I know why the Spartans are not afraid to die!"

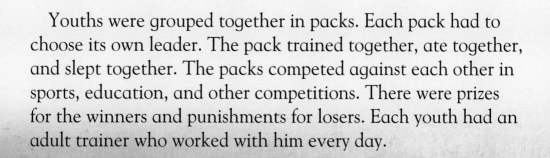

Youths were grouped together in packs. Each pack had to choose its own leader. The pack trained together, ate together, and slept together. The packs competed against each other in sports, education, and other competitions. There were prizes for the winners and punishments for losers. Each youth had an adult trainer who worked with him every day.

That's Fearless!

When one group of Spartan youths were told they were going to march to war, they broke out into loud cheers. Fighting a war would be easier than doing more training!

A close-up of a painting by Edgar Degas, *The Young Spartans,* shows a pack exercising before a competition.

Learning Skills and Getting Fit

All Spartan youths would practice for hours every day learning how to use weapons. The youths learned how to take steps of the same size as each other and to march in step with each other. Keeping in formation was vital to success in battle. This was known as the "Spartan step."

Youths took part in races called **hoplitodromos**. The races were run over a distance of about 430 yards (400 m) while wearing full armor! Bows could shoot arrows around the same distance, so this race was probably training for a battle against archers when the Spartans would need to dash forward as quickly as possible. From 520 BCE onwards the hoplitodromos was included in the Olympic Games.

FOREIGN YOUTHS

Each year a small number of youths from outside Sparta were allowed to join the agoge training camps. Hundreds applied, but only a dozen or so were accepted.

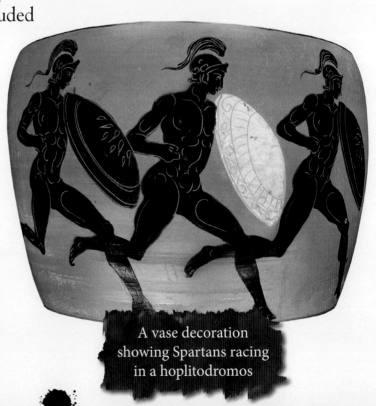

A vase decoration showing Spartans racing in a hoplitodromos

STARVING FOR STRENGTH

Spartans believed that hungry youths grew into tall men, well fed youths into short men. Youths were starved for days on end to try to make them grow tall!

The rival packs of youths would be made to fight battles against each other with blunted weapons. This taught them the sort of tactics they would use in the army. Injuries were common, but the youths were taught to ignore the pain and get back to training as soon as possible.

All youths were treated equally in the agoge. There were no privileges for the nobles or for the rich. The sons of the royal families were treated differently. They had to do extra lessons to learn the arts of diplomacy and government. The Spartans believed that it was important to teach the youths to be totally loyal to Sparta. They should have preferred to die than betray their country.

Young Spartans would learn about Spartan heroes. This statue shows King Menelaus holding the body of Patroclus after the famous battle of Troy.

Military Skills

A good Spartan soldier needed to know not only how to fight, but also how to survive on campaign and how to spy. He was taught how to cope with hunger, cold, and fatigue.

One important Spartan skill was how to draw maps. The youths would be taken on a march by their trainers. After the march they would have to draw a map of where they had gone. The maps didn't only show roads, buildings, and rivers. They also drew places that would make good camping areas, where horses could find grass to eat, and hills that would be easy to defend. Finding a place by reading maps was just as important.

HAIRY MEN

Adult Spartans didn't cut their hair. They brushed it daily and wore it in plaits, braids, or bunches. Some Spartans had hair reaching down to their waists!

Youths were expected to steal food from farms and houses. This taught them how to sneak around without being seen and how to break into property. They learned this skill so that they could find enough to eat when on campaign. If they were caught the youths were severely punished - not for stealing, but for being caught!

At the age of 18 the youths were put through exercises to test their skills with weapons, their strength, and their fitness. If they passed, the youths were given a special red cloak called a **phoinikis** and made part of the army. Those who came top were sent to join the **Hippeis**, the royal guard of 300 men. Men who failed the tests lost their status as Spartiates. They had to become periokoi, but often left Sparta, in shame, instead.

That's Fearless!

The Spartan army was called "The Walls." Sparta was the only city in Greece without defensive walls. The Spartans reckoned their army was so tough no enemy army would ever reach Sparta itself.

The walls of the city of Argos, in an area of Greece north of Sparta

Barrack life

When the young Spartans had finished their training they joined the adult barracks. The barracks were divided into houses of 32 men. A youth had to apply to join a house. He was only allowed to join if all the men in the house agreed. If a soldier had not been accepted into a house by the age of 30 he was expelled from Sparta!

The men in the house ate their meals together and marched to war together. When training for battle the houses were put together into groups of 4, each made up of 128 men. These **pentekostyes** worked together constantly to practice their fighting formations. The fact that the men knew each other well meant that they would trust each other in battle.

Four pentekostyes formed a **lochos** of 512 men. This was the basic formation of the Spartan army. All the houses of a lochos were located close to each other so that the men would get to know each other. The lochos would train together several times each month in order to perfect their fighting moves.

A Spartan lochos fighting together as one

KRYPTEIA

Some Spartans joined the **Krypteia**, a sort of secret police force. They camped out in hidden places in the countryside away from other Spartans. They patrolled the roads hunting bandits and watching foreigners. Any helot found out at night would be killed. They might also sneak into other countries to spy for invasion routes and camping grounds for the Spartan army.

All Spartan soldiers joined one of 27 sacred brotherhoods. These brotherhoods were responsible for organizing religious festivals, caring for temples, and ensuring that the gods were worshiped properly. The Spartans believed that they would win a battle only if the gods were satisfied. If there was a choice between fighting the enemy or holding a religious festival, the Spartans went to the temple.

The Spartans built simple temples often from wood, so they have not survived, unlike this Greek temple in Sicily, Italy, which still stands today.

The 300

When faced by a much larger enemy army, the Spartans would find a hilltop or pass where they could not be attacked from the sides.

BATTLE OF THERMOPYLAE

In August 480 BCE King Leonidas and his bodyguard of 300 Spartans guarded the narrow pass at Thermopylae against a vast Persian army of around 300,000 men. The pass was only about 164 feet (50 m) wide. Because of this the Persian forces could not enter the passage all at once. For three days Leonidas held the Persians. Then the Persians found a path over the mountain and attacked Leonidas from behind. All the Spartans were killed, but the delay allowed Sparta's allies to gather an army to defeat the Persians. After the war a monument was erected at Thermopylae which read "Passerby, go tell the Spartans that here we lie obedient to their wishes."

A statue of Leonidas at Thermopylae

Xerxes I
King of Persia

The 300 fighting
at Thermopylae

ANOTHER 300

In 546 BCE Sparta and Argos were at war over who should own the fertile Plain of Thyrea. It was agreed that 300 men from each side would fight at Thyrea to decide the issue. After fighting all day only one Spartan, Othryades, was still standing. The surviving Argos army were too frightened to face him and fled. Because Othryades occupied the field of battle, and stripped the enemy dead of their armor, Sparta was declared the winner and occupied Thyrea!

Armor

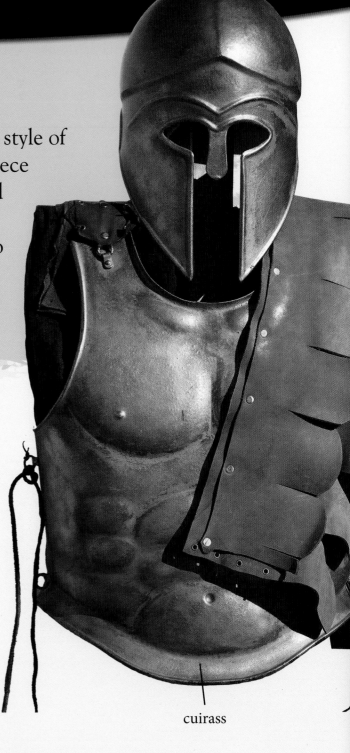

The Spartans perfected a style of warfare common in Greece based on a foot soldier called the **hoplite**. Hoplites were heavily armored soldiers who fought shoulder to shoulder in formations of hundreds or even thousands of men.

Their helmet was made from a single sheet of bronze, so that it had no weak joins or cracks. From about 800 BCE the Spartans used a type of helmet first used in Corinth. The **Corinthian helmet** covered the face and neck, with a small gap for the eyes and mouth.

On their body they wore a bronze armor called a **cuirass**. Sometimes the armor was shaped to look like the muscles of the body.

cuirass

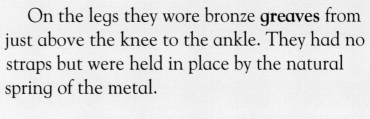

On the legs they wore bronze **greaves** from just above the knee to the ankle. They had no straps but were held in place by the natural spring of the metal.

Spartan shields were round, and about 3.3 feet (1 m) across. They were made of several thin layers of wood glued together alternating with leather to produce a strong, light shield that was flexible enough to absorb blows without shattering. The shield was faced by a thin sheet of bronze to deflect pointed weapons.

back of a greave showing how well they fit on the leg

FATAL MISTAKE

Spartan soldiers painted the Greek letter lambda on their shields. Troops from Messina tricked their way into the city of Elis by painting the same design on their shields. The men guarding the gates of Elis thought the soldiers were from their ally Sparta, not their enemy Messina!

A Spartan shield with the Greek letter lambda on

In Combat

The Spartan hoplites were ferocious killers in battle. They slaughtered their enemies in large numbers during a battle and finished off the badly wounded rather than treat their enemies' wounds. They took prisoners only after a battle had ended, not during one.

The spear was the main weapon used by the Spartans. The spearhead was made of iron and shaped like a tree leaf. The point and sides were sharpened regularly to make sure it was always ready for use.

Spartan soldiers had a short sword about 16 inches (40 cm) long called a **xiphos**. The weapon had a straight blade that bulged out near the tip. It could be used both to stab or to slash. The sword was used if the spear broke in battle.

Actaeon using a xiphos sword

That's Fearless!

A Persian envoy once asked King Agesilaus of Sparta why Spartan swords were so short. "We fight closer to the enemy than you do," replied Agesilaus.

LIZARD KILLER

The bronze spike at the other end of the spear was called the **sauroter** or "lizard-killer." It was used to kill wounded enemy soldiers as the army marched over them.

sauroter

spearhead

The Spartans used other types of soldiers from cities allied to Sparta because Spartans considered anything other than hand to hand combat beneath them! **Peltasts** had no armor except a small wicker shield. They threw javelins at the enemy from a distance. **Skiritai** had swords and long spears. They patrolled the camps at night and searched the woods where enemies might be hiding. On horseback, the Spartan cavalry scouted ahead of the marching army, looking for a good place to camp for the night, and trying to discover where the enemy army was.

New Methods of Warfare

After about the year 440 BCE Spartan armies began to fight wars in a new style. Instead of standing in solid groups, Spartans began to move quickly about the battlefield in more flexible formations. They also began fighting wars further away from Sparta itself. The new type of fighting needed new types of equipment.

The old-style Corinthian helmet covered the ears, so soldiers could not hear shouted orders easily. Spartans changed to a new style called the **pilos** helmet. This was shaped like a pointed cone with a broad flange around the base. It left the ears free and allowed the soldier to see to the sides more easily.

pilos helmet

That's Fearless!

In 362 BCE the Thebans launched a surprise attack on a Spartan camp. Spartan soldier Isidas leapt from his campbed, grabbed his spear and shield and ran naked into battle. His general gave him a top award for bravery, then fined him a huge sum of money for going into battle without the proper clothing!

A mosaic showing Alexander the Great wearing linen armor

The metal cuirass was replaced by one made of linen. Up to 18 layers of linen were glued and sewn together, then cut to shape. This armor could stop an arrow or sword, but not a spear thrust. It was much lighter than bronze armor. The Spartans could run more quickly about the battlefield and march longer distances. By about 350 BCE Spartans stopped wearing body armor at all. They were protected only by a shield and helmet.

Spartan officers had a special "T" shaped staff. Otherwise the senior officers were dressed and equipped exactly the same as the ordinary soldiers. Spartans prized equality among Spartiates.

HAIRSTYLES

Spartan hairstyles changed too. Spartans began to plait their long hair into eight braids. Four braids fell in front of the shoulders and four behind. They also shaved off their mustaches, though they kept their beards.

Trickery

If the Spartans felt they couldn't win a battle, they would often trick the enemy instead.

USING TRICKERY ON MOUNT IRA

In 678 BCE a Spartan army laid siege to the Messenian fortress of Mount Ira. After ten years the Spartans realized that they couldn't capture the fortress. They offered to let the Messenians leave freely if they wanted to. When the Messenians marched away the Spartans captured the fortress!

That's Fearless!

In 479 BCE an army of about 80,000 Greeks and 10,000 Spartans was ambushed by twice as many Persian soldiers at Plataea. The Spartan Pausanias sacrificed a goat to the goddess Hera. The priest said that the omens were good. The Spartans charged forward as all the other Greeks retreated. They smashed through the center of the Persian army, encouraging the other Greeks to turn and fight. Only 43,000 Persians escaped, the rest were killed or were taken as slaves.

GETTING ENEMY HELP

In 457 BCE a force of 1,500 Spartans had traveled to northern Greece to interfere in a dispute between two of her allies. Returning home, an army of 14,000 Athenians blocked their route at Tanagra. Prince Nicomedes of Sparta waited for the Athenians to attack. The Athenians suffered heavy losses. A group of Thessalian cavalry from the Athenian army changed to the Spartan side during the battle! Nicomedes attacked and smashed the enemy. The Spartans could then march home!

The Thessalians were considered the finest cavalry of Greece.

The sacred groves of ancient Greece were believed to link the human world with the world of the gods. Animals would be sacrificed on an altar there.

DINNERTIME!

In 494 BCE about 5,000 Spartans under King Cleomenes faced 10,000 **Argives** at Sepeia. All day the two armies stared at each other, but as dusk fell the Spartans went to eat dinner. It was a trick, as soon as the Argives relaxed, the Spartans attacked. Some Argives tried to hide in the Sacred Grove of Argos. Cleomenes disregarded the tradition of sanctuary and killed them. However, when he approached Argos, Cleomenes saw it was guarded by boys, old men, and women. As it would be seen as a disgrace to attack them, Cleomenes made peace.

The basic formation of the Spartan army was the **phalanx**. It was used by other Greek armies as well, but it was the Spartans who perfected the use of the formation in battle.

The basic phalanx was made up of men in hoplite armor. The men stood close together. Each man took up about 3.3 feet (1 m) of frontage. There were usually eight ranks of men lined up one behind one another. When moving over the battlefield the ranks were 6.6 feet (2 m) apart. When fighting another phalanx the ranks closed up, so that the shield of each man was pushing into the back of the man in front.

That's Fearless!

Some soldier allies of Sparta mocked a Spartan soldier who had a deformed leg and was limping. He glared at them and replied. "All I need to do in battle is stand firm in the phalanx, I won't need to run away."

The youngest, strongest men were put in the front of the phalanx. In this position they could stab forward with their spears, over the tops of shields to kill or wound men at the front of the enemy phalanx. The older, experienced men went at the back of the phalanx. They were less likely to run away than younger men and so could keep the phalanx in action for longer.

Every man in the phalanx tried to push forward. If they could build up momentum the enemy would be forced to fight while stepping backward, which made them more likely to trip over or fall down. If a phalanx was moving back quickly it was more likely to break up and for the men to flee.

When facing cavalry, the rear four ranks would squeeze between the men in the front four ranks. This meant each man occupied only 1 1/2 feet (50 cm) of front. The shields of the front rank overlapped to form a solid wall. The spears were held forward to form a solid hedge of spikes that the horses would shy away from.

A Change in Tactics

By 600 BCE the Spartans had become so effective in phalanx battles that very few other cities dared to face it in war! The cities around Sparta formed the Peloponnesian League, which was led by Sparta. After 500 BCE new ways of fighting battles were developed in Greece, and Sparta had to develop new battle tactics to remain successful.

The long charge was used when facing enemy troops equipped with bows or javelins. Using this system the Spartans would halt when just out of range of the enemy missiles. On the word of command the Spartans would run forwards with their shields held in front of them. When they reached the enemy the Spartans did not stop but crashed straight into them, seeking to knock them over so they could be killed with the sauroter.

A diagonal phalanx was formed with one part of the phalanx pushed ahead of the rest. Usually this section faced the weakest part of the enemy line. The forward section would drive through the enemy line, disrupt them and lead to an easy victory.

In an echelon attack, one section of the phalanx was much deeper than the rest. The section might have 16 or 32 ranks of men. The men in this stronger section would push forward like a living battering ram to drive a hole in the enemy line!

A rolling attack took place once a hole had been driven in the enemy line. Instead of chasing the fleeing enemy, the Spartans reformed their phalanx to face sideways, then attacked the flank or rear of the remaining enemy troops.

a traditional phalanx

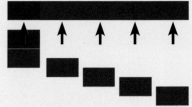

a diagonal phalanx

an echelon attack

▬ = strongest troops

THE TEARLESS BATTLE

In 368 BCE a Spartan army defeated an Arcadian army without losing a single man! The Spartans advanced, then stopped at about 160 feet (50 m) from the enemy. All the Spartans gave a loud shout and charged. The entire Arcadian army promptly turned and fled! The Spartans dubbed it "the Tearless Battle."

That's Fearless!

In 401 BCE the Spartan general Clearchus was negotiating a treaty with King Artaxerxes of Persia when he was imprisoned. When told he would be executed, Clearchus asked for a comb so he could make his hair and beard neat for the event.

Spartan Discipline

Although all Spartiates were equal in law, the Spartan army depended on absolute discipline in battle for its success. The Spartiates were willing to follow orders from their commanders because they all shared in making decisions about the state. They also believed in a strict code of honor.

Sparta was ruled by a Council of 28 men over the age of 60. When one died, a replacement was elected. All Spartiates could vote for the new member. If the Council wanted to introduce a new law, declare war, or spend money they would call a meeting of the Spartiates.

Sparta had two kings, one from each royal family. The kings supervised meetings of the Council and the Spartiates. The kings were the chief priests of Sparta and officiated at major religious festivals. They also acted as appeal judges in legal matters. When Sparta was at war, one king stayed at home while the other led the army.

King Leonidas II sending his son-in-law into exile

Punishments in the Spartan army were designed to embarrass, not hurt. A man who disobeyed his commander was forced to stand fully armed all night. A soldier who was found guilty of cowardice lost all his rights. He had to wear a white cloak with colored patches sewn on it. He could not get married, own land, or hold public office!

The Spartan code of honor was harsh. The soldier Aristodemus missed a battle because an eye infection, meaning he could not see. He insisted that he lead the charge at the next battle to make up for this, and was killed doing so. In fact, a Spartiates aim was to die "the beautiful death," killed in battle facing the enemy.

If a man dropped his shield, he then had to carry it over his head.

That's Fearless!

In 480 BCE a refugee fleeing from the advancing Persian army told the Spartan commander Dienekes that the Persians had so many archers their arrows would blot out the sun. "That's nice," replied Dienekes. "We'll be able to fight in the shade."

ASKING QUESTIONS

When on campaign any soldier had the right to question his officers. Even the king had to answer to his men. The Spartan men were therefore confident that their commanders knew what they were doing. But once the enemy was in sight, strict obedience was enforced.

The Phalanx

Fighting in a phalanx required bravery and discipline. Nobody did it better than the Spartans.

TAYGETOS

Mount Taygetos

In 739 BCE Sparta and Messenia were at war over disputed border territory on Mount Taygetos. The Spartan King Polydorus organized his heavily armored infantry into a dense formation several ranks deep. This is the first time a phalanx was used in Greek warfare, and it seems to have been a Spartan invention. The Messenians attacked, led by Euphaes, in the traditional style with archers, lightly armed men, and hoplites all mixed together in one formation. The disciplined Spartan phalanx was unbreakable and the Spartans won the battle.

MANTINEA

A phalanx can be defeated! In 362 BCE King Agesilaus II led an army of Spartans and allies to attack the Thebans and their allies led by Epaminondas. The Thebans attacked using a different phalanx tactic. Instead of dividing their army equally across the phalanx, the stronger part of their army attacked the Spartans on the left. The Spartans retreated, and the rest of their army fell back as well. Then Epaminondas was killed, and the battle ended with both sides claiming the victory!

A vase with an image of a Spartan battle

CORONEA

In 394 BCE an army of 15,000 Spartans and their allies was marching toward Sparta when their route was blocked by 20,000 Thebans, Argives, and others. King Agesilaus II formed his men into a phalanx and advanced. The Argives fled and left the Thebans by themselves. The Spartans turned on the Thebans and charged a second time. The Thebans stood and fought, and more than half their army were killed. The Spartans lost only 350 men.

That's Fearless!

In 346 BCE King Philip II of Macedon defeated an alliance of Greek states and demanded that all Greek cities submit to him. The message he sent to Sparta was "You must submit to me at once, for if I bring my army into your land, I will destroy your farms, slay your people, and burn your city." The Spartans sent back an answer made up of a single word "if!"

Warrior Kings

Leonidas

King Leonidas I was born about 540 BCE, but as he had three elder brothers he did not expect to become king. He trained as a soldier in the agoge and fought in several battles, including the Battle of Sepeia. Two of his elder brothers died. His third brother Cleomenes I, went insane and was removed from the throne. Leonidas therefore became king at the age of 59! The next year he led the Spartan army to the Battle of Thermopylae, where he was killed.

King Leonidas' statue at Thermopylae

LEOTYCHIDAS

King Leotychidas ruled alongside King Leonidas I. When Leonidas marched to Thermopylae, Leotychidas remained at home. He defeated the Persians at Mycale in 479 BCE, but three years later he allowed Persian allies to escape from Thessaly. He was sent into exile as punishment until his death.

Menelaus

According to legend Menelaus was King of Sparta in about 1300 BCE. Menelaus married Helen, the most beautiful woman in the world. When Helen ran off to live with Prince Paris of Troy, Menelaus raised a vast army and attacked Troy. The Trojan War that followed was famous for the Trojan Horse and the heroism of Achilles.

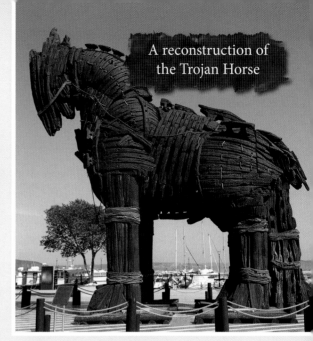

A reconstruction of the Trojan Horse

Agesilaus II

Small in height and lame from birth King Agesilaus II ruled as one of the two kings of Sparta from 400 to 360 BCE. He led an army to what is now Turkey to help Greek cities there fight against the **Persian Empire**. He won several battles, then returned to Sparta to lead the army in a war against Corinth and Athens. Although he won every battle he fought, Agesilaus was a poor diplomat so Sparta ended up weaker than when he became king.

That's Fearless!

Nabis became king of Sparta in 207 BCE when the Roman Empire was expanding into Greece. He tried to modernize Sparta by giving the helots new rights and increasing trade. This made Sparta wealthy and powerful, which made Rome attack them! Nabis was killed in battle in 192 BCE.

Nabis II, the last king of Sparta

Brave Leaders

Brasidas

Brasidas fought several battles against Athens. His greatest victory was at Lyncestis in 423 BCE when he escaped an ambush, and turned around to defeat the enemy. He was famous for leading his men on swift marches to take the enemy by surprise and for attacks from unexpected directions. He was killed in battle at Amphipolis in 422 BCE. Sparta held an annual festival in his honor!

Brasidas captured Amphipolis from the Athenians. Athens tried to retake it. Brasidas tricked their army into camping on Mount Kerdyllium where he could easily attack them. Brasidas' army won but he was one of the few Spartans that was killed.

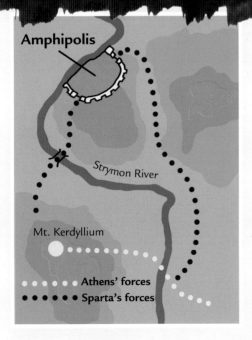

Amphipolis

Strymon River

Mt. Kerdyllium

○ ○ ○ ○ ○ Athens' forces
● ● ● ● ● Sparta's forces

LYSANDER

The Spartan naval commander Lysander was born about 450 BCE into a noble but poor family. Although he trained to be a soldier, Lysander was given the task of creating a Spartan navy. The following year he defeated Athens at the Battle of Notium, and later beat them again at Aegospotami, forcing Athens to make peace. He was killed at the Battle of Halliartus in 395 BCE fighting against Thebes.

While most Greek women stayed at home to care for their families, many Spartan women went to war.

Queen Gorgo

Gorgo was the clever daughter of King Cleomenes and married King Leonidas. Greeks wrote using writing tablets made of wood covered in wax. The message was written in the wax, and after it was read it could be wiped smooth for a new message. One day a blank tablet arrived for Leonidas. Gorgo realized there must be a secret message written on the wood underneath the wax. It was a warning that the Persians were about to attack!

That's Fearless!

The Spartan woman Hydna was famous as a swimmer and athlete. In 480 BCE she swam more than 10 miles (16 km) to where the Persian fleet was at anchor. Diving down, she cut the ropes securing the ships. The ships drifted onto rocks and were wrecked.

QUEEN ARACHIDAMIA

Sparta was attacked by the vast army of Pyrrhus of Epirus. The Spartan council was debating whether or not to send the women and children to safety in Crete. Queen Arachidamia heard about the debate. She marched into the council chamber with a sword in her hand and demanded "How am I expected to survive the death of my city?" The women stayed. Arachidamia led a unit of women warriors in the subsequent battle and Pyrrhus was defeated!

Spartan Timeline

The term BCE stands for "before the Christian era" and measures time before our modern calendar began. If you see AD before a date that means it is a year in our calendar. Anything that happened before AD 1 will have BCE written after it. Years before AD 1 go backward rather than forward, so 100 BCE is one hundred years after 200 BCE!

- **c.1600 BCE Sparta Is Founded**
  According to legend, Sparta was founded by Lelex, the son of the sea god Poseidon, and Epaphos, princess of Egypt. Archaeology shows that the earliest settlement in Sparta was around this time.

2000 BCE

1500 BCE

Paris taking Helen from Sparta

- **c.1250 BCE
  The Trojan War**
  The famous Trojan War is believed to have begun when Helen, Queen of Sparta, ran off to live with Prince Paris of Troy. King Menelaos of Sparta raised a mighty army of allied Greek cities to sail to Asia Minor to lay siege to Troy.

c.930 BCE The Kings of Sparta

The rule of Sparta is divided between two royal families, both descended from the mythical hero Heracles (Hercules). Although dates are unclear, the history of Sparta is usually thought to start from this event.

A marble head of Heracles

1000 BCE

c.780 BCE Lycurgus

The exiled prince Lycurgus returned to Sparta and undertook a major reform of the city. He began the social system that allowed a small elite to train full time for war. The system changed in small ways over time but remained basically the same for over 600 years!

500 BCE

546 BCE
The Peloponnesian League

After the Battle of the Champions, Sparta became leader of the Peloponnesian League. This alliance of cities and states in southern Greece became the most powerful alliance in Greece.

The lush, green Pamisos valley

685 BCE - 668 BCE
Second Messenian War

Sparta conquered rich and wealthy Messenia and the fertile valley of the Pamisos. The captured inhabitants were made into helots. The conquest brought wealth to Sparta.

490 BCE Persian Wars
The wars between the Greek states and the Persian Empire began in 490 BCE. Sparta was involved in the great battles of Thermopylae, Plataea, and Mycale as well as many smaller battles.

The 464 BCE earthquake's epicenter was in Sparta.

464 BCE The Spartan Earthquake
Around 20,000 people were killed by a powerful earthquake in Sparta. The damage to the wealth, population, and buildings of Sparta was devastating. Sparta never fully recovered.

400 BCE

500 BCE

460 BCE War with Athens
Rivalry with Athens led to war in 460 BCE when Athens tried to take advantage of Sparta's weakness after the earthquake. The wars continued off and on until 404 BCE when Sparta finally captured Athens and imposed a peace treaty.

- **371 BCE Battle of Leuctra**
The Spartan army was defeated in open battle for the first time ever. The victor, Epaminondas of Thebes, had developed a new tactic known as the echelon attack. Sparta suffered a blow to its fearless reputation and lost its power outside the Peloponnesian League.

That's Fearless!

In 480 BCE at the Battle of Thermopylae a force of 300 Spartans faced an army of about 300,000 Persians.

- **272 BCE Siege of Sparta**
King Pyrrhus of Epirus led his army to attack Sparta and laid siege to the city. The women of Sparta joined the defense and help drive off Epirus. This was the first time that Sparta itself had ever been attacked.

300 BCE

200 BCE

- **331 BCE Alexander the Great**
Alexander the Great of Macedon tried to force all Greek states to pay tribute to Macedon. Sparta refused.

- **146 BCE Defeat by Rome**
In 146 BCE a huge Roman army invaded Greece. The small Spartan army was crushed at the Battle of Corinth. Sparta became part of the Roman Empire.

A statue of Alexander the Great

What Do You Know?

Can you answer these questions about the Spartans?

1. When was Sparta founded?

2. Which Spartan woman wrecked dozens of Persian ships?

3. Which Spartan queen is remembered for her skills at reading secret messages?

4. What was the favorite food in Sparta?

5. How large was a Spartan shield?

6. When did a Spartan boy begin training to be a soldier?

7. What was the name of the Spartan military training system?

8. Who wrote the songs sung by Spartans on the march and in battle?

9. Who commanded the 300 Spartans at the Battle of Thermopylae?

10. According to King Agesilaus, why did Spartans use unusually short swords?

Answers on page 48

Further Information

Books

Blake, Chris. *Greek Warriors* (Time Hunters.) New York, NY: HarperCollins Children's Books, 2013.

Cowles, Julia. *Our Little Spartan Cousin.* Chapel Hill, NC: Yesterday's Classics, 2008.

Green, John. *Sparta!* (Warriors of the Ancient World). Mineola, NY: Dover Children's, 2013.

McLeese, Don. *Spartans* (Warriors Graphic Illustrated). Vero Beach, FL: Rourke Publishing, 2011.

Websites

BBC Education page on Sparta
http://www.bbc.co.uk/schools/primaryhistory/ancient_greeks/sparta/

Ducksters page on ancient Greece
http://www.ducksters.com/history/ancient_greece.php

Primary Homework page on ancient Greece
http://www.primaryhomeworkhelp.co.uk/Greece.html

Publisher's note to educators and parents: Our editors have carefully reviewed these websites to ensure that they are suitable for students. Many websites change frequently, however, and we cannot guarantee that a site's future contents will continue to meet our high standards of quality and educational value. Be advised that students should be closely supervised whenever they access the Internet.

Glossary

agoge The military training system of Sparta through which all Spartiate boys were put. Those who failed were expelled from the Spartiate class.

Argive A person from the city of Argos.

Corinthian helmet A style of helmet developed in Corinth. It covered the entire head down to the neck and was sometimes topped by a plume or crest.

cuirass A type of body armor made from one sheet of metal that covered the front from waist to neck. A second sheet sometimes covered the back as well.

greaves Armor designed to protect the shins.

helots The bottom social class in Sparta. Helots were forced to work on farms, could be killed if they went out after dark and had very few social rights.

Hippeis The royal bodyguard of 300 men. Only the very best fighters were invited to join the Hippeis.

hoplite A type of soldier who carried a large round shield, helmet, and spear, and who was trained to fight in the phalanx formation.

hoplitodromos A sport that involved running a distance of about 430 yards (400 m) while wearing full armor.

Krypteia The combined police and spy service of Sparta.

lochos A group of 512 men, the smallest unit sent to war and able to operate on its own.

Peltast A type of soldier without armor equipped with shield and javelins.

pentekostyes A group of 128 men, the basic tactical unit of the Spartan army.

periokoi The middle social class in Sparta. They included families running businesses, farms, or trading with other countries.

Persian Empire A powerful empire that stretched from what is now Turkey to northern India and included Egypt and parts of Arabia.

phalanx A dense formation of armored men standing shoulder to shoulder and standing about eight ranks deep.

phoinikis The large red cloak woven from wool that was worn by all Spartan soldiers.

pilos A style of helmet that covered only the top of the head, leaving the face and ears free.

pyrriche A dance performed by Spartan boys training to become soldiers, it involved juggling with razor-sharp weapons.

sauroter The bronze spike on the butt of a spear used to stick the spear in the ground or to kill wounded enemy soldiers.

Skiritai A type of soldier armed with a sword and spear.

Spartiates The top social class in Sparta. Only Spartiates were allowed to join the army.

xiphos A small sword carried by all Spartan soldiers for them to use if their spear broke.

Index

Answers to Quiz

1. around 1600 BCE
2. Hydna
3. Queen Gorgo. She realized you could hide a secret message underneath the wax on a tablet
4. black soup - made by boiling pork and barley in pig's blood and vinegar
5. about 3.3 feet (1 m) across
6. at the age of five years
7. the agoge
8. Tyrtaios
9. King Leonidas
10. So that they could fight closer to the enemy